COURAGE AT THE DENTIST

By Wynette Turner, Michael J. Clark & Jasmine L. Clark

Illustrations by Zeynep Zahide Cakmak

Copyright © 2020 Wynette Turner, Michael J. Clark and Jasmine L. Clark

All rights reserved. No part of this book may be used or reproduced in any manner whatsoever without the prior written permission of the author.

This book is dedicated to my daughter Jasmine L. Clark for having courage throughout all her dental appointments. It is also dedicated to all the little children who want to be strong and courageous while at the dentist.

This book belongs to:
_____

Hi I'm Sarena!
Do you know what courage is?

Courage is having the strength
to make good choices even when I am afraid.

I have the courage to go to the dentist to get my teeth cleaned.
I used to be afraid, but I am not anymore!

I HAVE COURAGE!

It is ok to be a little scared,
but the dentist will be right there with you.

One day, I had to go to the dentist to get
not 1,
not 2,
but 3
teeth pulled out!

The dentist needed to get those baby teeth out of my mouth,

so that my big girl teeth can grow.

Sometimes, teeth come out on their own,
and sometimes they need a little help.
Three of my teeth just would not come out,
so they need a little help.

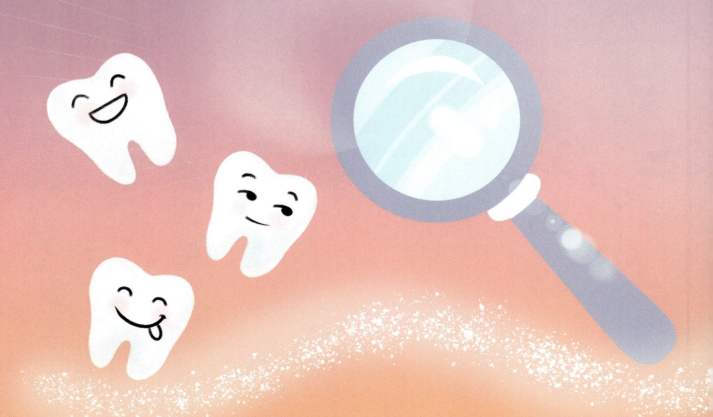

At first, I was a little scared and could feel my mouth and body shaking. I started to cry a little.

My mommy and brother were in the waiting room. I was in this colorful and bright room with shiny tools and a Tv.

My dentist talked to me, so that I could feel better.

But I was still a little scared,

then I remembered...

I am ready!
I have courage!
I can do it!

I am ready!
I have courage!
I can do it!

So if I can do it, you can too!

And remember these words!

You are ready!
You have courage!
You can do it!